# The Ball That Wouldn't Bounce

ISBN 979-8-89130-498-7 (paperback)
ISBN 979-8-89130-499-4 (digital)



Christian Faith Publishing
832 Park Avenue
Meadville, PA 16335
www.christianfaithpublishing.com

Printed in the United States of America

# The Ball That Wouldn't Bounce

Josie Wheaton

L iving in a small town, next door to each other, were two boys Brandon and Billy. They were best friends and did everything together. They had the best time together going for walks in the woods or going swimming in the pond. No matter where they were, their parents always knew they were together.

The town was having its annual summer celebration at the fairgrounds. Some of the activities included a pie-tasting contest, a jump-rope contest, and a ball-bouncing contest.

Brandon and Billy were interested in the ball-bouncing contest. The person who bounced their ball the highest would win the prize.

SUMMER CELEBRATION
Pie Tasting
Jump Rope
Ball Bouncing

Brandon and Billy practiced by bouncing their ball every day.

Brandon knew that Billy's ball was bouncing higher than his. Brandon really wanted to win the contest. So he asked Billy for his ball, and when Billy gave it to him, Brandon put a hole in it.

Every time Billy bounced his ball, air would come out of it. When air comes out of a ball, it loses its bounce.

Brandon said, "Let's not bounce our balls anymore today as we should let them rest. The contest is tomorrow, and we want to be ready for it."

The next day, Brandon and Billy went to the fair together. There were twenty people signed up for the ball-bouncing contest. They waited in line until it was their turn.

BALL BOUNCING CONTEST
PIE EATING CONTEST
JUMP ROPE CONTEST

1st

When Brandon bounced his ball, it went higher and higher, every time he bounced it. Billy had trouble bouncing his ball. He bounced his ball over and over trying harder and harder each time to make it go higher. No matter what Billy did, his ball would not bounce high. Billy wanted to cry.

When the contest was over, the judge announced the winner— it was Brandon. Brandon's prize was two free tickets to the movie theater in town.

Billy was sad because his ball wouldn't bounce, but he was happy that his best friend Brandon won the contest. Billy congratulated Brandon on his win.

Brandon knew what he did to Billy's ball was wrong. That night, when Brandon said his bedtime prayers, he talked to Jesus about what he did. He told Jesus that he put a hole in Billy's ball. "Dear Jesus, I don't know why I cheated. I hurt Billy, my best friend. How could I have been so bad? I don't know what to do. I need you to help me, Jesus." Brandon couldn't forgive himself for what he had done, but he was hoping and praying that Jesus would forgive him.

Jesus thanked Brandon for turning to Him and said, "I see and hear everything. I saw what you did to your friends' ball. When you go tell Billy what you did, and ask for his forgiveness, I too will forgive you!"

1st
BIBLE

Brandon couldn't sleep well that night because he kept thinking about the hurt he had caused his best friend Billy.

Brandon remembered back to a day when they were in the woods, and he twisted his ankle. Brandon couldn't walk because it hurt, and Billy ran to get help for him.

Brandon also remembered a time they were at the pond. While swimming, Brandon got a cramp in his leg and couldn't move to safety. Billy jumped in and pulled Brandon out of the pond. Billy has always been there for Brandon.

The next day, Brandon walked over to Billy's house to talk to him. He told Billy that he put a hole in his ball, and he didn't win because every time he bounced the ball, air came out. This prevented the ball from bouncing high. "Billy, you have been my very best friend, and I don't know why I did what I did. I can't change what I did. I wish I could. I'm so ashamed of myself for hurting you," Brandon said with tears in his eyes.

"The theater tickets aren't worth my losing you. There is nothing in this world worth losing our friendship over!" He continued, "I prayed to Jesus last night telling Him what I did. I told Him how sorry I was and that I never ever wanted to hurt you again. I am so sorry, Billy. Please forgive me!"

Billy told Brandon that we all do things that hurt others sometimes. Brandon turned to Jesus, and Billy knows that Jesus doesn't turn anyone away. "Thank you for turning to Jesus! He has forgiven you Brandon, and so have I."

Brandon gave Billy the theater tickets and told him that he would have won, so the prize was his. Billy didn't want the tickets; he had a better idea. Billy and Brandon went to the theater together. When they arrived at the theater, the person taking the tickets told them that free popcorn and drinks were included. Billy and Brandon enjoyed the movie, and the best part of all was they were together, best friends again!

POP CORN
DR INKS
20

# About the Author

Josie Wheaton is a mom, grandma, and great-grandma who loves Jesus and wants to share that love with the generations to come.